GW00514772

Benedict XVI

The Holy Shroud
An Icon of Love

Pastoral Visit to Turin
2 May 2010

*All booklets are published thanks to the
generous support of the members of the
Catholic Truth Society*

CATHOLIC TRUTH SOCIETY
PUBLISHERS TO THE HOLY SEE

Contents

A civilization of love 3

Spiritual renewal 11

True freedom: a view to the "forever" 13

An Icon written in blood 20

Suffering and redemption 26

A civilization of love

I am happy to be with you on this festive day and to celebrate this solemn Eucharist for you. I greet everyone present and in particular the Pastor of your Archdiocese, Cardinal Severino Poletto, whom I thank for his warm words to me on behalf of all. I also greet the Archbishops and Bishops present, the priests, the men and women religious and the representatives of the Ecclesial Associations and Movements. I address a respectful thought to Hon. Mr Sergio Chiamparino, the Mayor, with gratitude for his kind greeting, to the representatives of the Government and to the civil and military Authorities, with special thanks to those who have generously offered their cooperation for this Pastoral Visit. I extend my thoughts to those who are unable to be present, especially the sick, the lonely and all those in difficulty. I entrust the City of Turin and all its inhabitants to the Lord in this Eucharistic celebration, which, as it does every Sunday, invites us to partake as a community in the twofold banquet of the Word of truth and the Bread of eternal life.

Glorification in the passion

We are in the Easter Season which is the time of Jesus' glorification. The Gospel we have just heard reminds us that this glorification is brought about in the Passion. In the Paschal Mystery, passion and glorification are closely bound together and form an indissoluble unity. When Judas leaves the Upper Room to carry out his scheme of betrayal that will lead to the Master's death, Jesus says: "now is the Son of man glorified, and in him God is glorified" (*Jn* 13:31): the glorification of Jesus begins at that very moment. The Evangelist John makes it quite clear: he does not in fact say that Jesus was glorified only after his Passion, through his Resurrection; rather he shows that precisely with the Passion his glorification began. In it Jesus manifests his glory, which is the glory of love, which gives itself totally. He loved the Father, doing his will to the very end, with a perfect gift of self; he loved humanity, giving his life for us. Thus he was already glorified in his Passion and God was glorified in him. But the Passion as a very real and profound expression of his love is only a beginning. This is why Jesus says that his glorification is also to come (cf. *ibid.*, 13: 32). Then, when he announces his departure from this world (cf. *ibid.*, 13: 33), the Lord gives his disciples a new commandment, as it were a testament, so that they might continue his presence among them in a new way: "A new commandment I give to you, that you love one another; even as I have loved you, that you also love one another" (*Jn* 13:34). If we love each other, Jesus will continue to be present in our midst, to be glorified in this world.

Progress in love

Jesus speaks of a "new commandment". But what is new about it? In the Old Testament, God had already given the commandment of love; but this commandment has become new now because Jesus makes a very important addition to it: "*As I have loved you*, that you also love one another". What is new is precisely this "loving as Jesus loved". All our loving is preceded by his love and refers to this love, it fits into this love and is achieved precisely through this love. The Old Testament did not present any model of love; it only formulated the precept of love. Instead, Jesus gave himself to us as a model and source of love a boundless, universal love that could transform all negative circumstances and all obstacles into opportunities to progress in love. And in this City's Saints we see the fulfilment of this love, always from the source of Jesus' love.

Holiness and service

In past centuries, the Church in Turin had a rich tradition of holiness and generous service to the brethren as both the Cardinal Archbishop and Mr Mayor pointed out thanks to the work of zealous priests and men and women religious of both active and contemplative life and faithful laypeople. Jesus' words thus acquire a special resonance for this Church of Turin, a generous and active Church, beginning with her priests. In giving us the new commandment, Jesus asks us to live his own love and on his own love, which is the truly credible, eloquent and effective sign for proclaiming the coming of the Kingdom of God to the world. Clearly, with our own strength alone we are weak and limited. In us there is always a resistance to love and in our existence there are very many difficulties that cause division, resentment and ill will. However, the Lord promised us that he would be present in our lives, making us capable of this generous, total love that can overcome all obstacles, even those in our own hearts. If we are united to Christ, we can truly love in this way. Loving others as Jesus loved us is only possible with that power which is communicated to us in the relationship with him, especially in the Eucharist, in which his Sacrifice of love that generates love becomes really present: this is the true newness in the world and the power of a permanent glorification of God who is glorified in the continuity of the love of Jesus in our love.

Labourers in the vineyard

I would therefore like to say a word of encouragement especially to the Priests and Deacons of this Church, who dedicate themselves generously to pastoral work, as well as to the men and women Religious. Being a labourer in the Lord's vineyard can sometimes be tiring, duties increase, there are so many demands and problems are not lacking: may you be able to draw daily from this relationship of love with God in prayer the strength to transmit the prophetic announcement of salvation; refocus your existence on what is essential in the Gospel; cultivate a real dimension of communion and brotherhood in the presbyterate, in your communities, in your relations with the People of God; bear witness in your ministry to the power of love that comes from on high, that comes from the Lord present in our midst.

Courage in the community

The First Reading we have heard presents to us precisely a special way of glorifying Jesus: the apostolate and its fruits. Paul and Barnabas, at the end of their first apostolic voyage, return to the cities they have already visited and give fresh courage to the disciples, exhorting them to remain firm in the faith for, as they say, "through many tribulations we must enter the kingdom of God" (*Ac* 14:22). Christian life, dear brothers and sisters, is not easy; I know that difficulties, problems and anxieties abound in Turin: I am thinking in particular of those who currently live in precarious conditions, because of the scarcity of work, uncertainty about the future, physical and moral suffering. I am thinking of families, of young people, of elderly people who often live alone, of the marginalized and of immigrants. Yes, life leads to confrontation with many difficulties, many problems, but it is precisely the certainty that comes from faith, the certainty that we are not alone, that God loves each one without distinction and is close to everyone with his love, that makes it possible to face, live through and surmount the effort of dealing with daily problems. It was the universal love of the Risen Christ that motivated the Apostles to come out of themselves, to disseminate the word of God, to spend themselves without reserve for others, with courage, joy and serenity. The Risen One has a power of love that overcomes every limit, that does not stop in front of any obstacle. And the Christian community, especially in the most pastorally demanding situations, must be a concrete instrument of this love of God.

Strength in witness

I urge families to live the Christian dimension of love in simple everyday actions in family relationships, overcoming divisions and misunderstandings; in cultivating the faith, which makes communion even stronger. Nor, in the rich and diverse world of the university and of culture, should there be a lack of the witness to love of which today's Gospel speaks in the capacity for attentive listening and humble dialogue in the search for Truth, in the certainty that Truth itself will come to us and catch hold of us. I would also like to encourage the frequently difficult endeavours of those called to administer public affairs: collaboration in order to achieve the common good and to make the City ever more human and liveable is a sign that

Christian thought on man is never contrary to his freedom but favours a greater fullness that can only find its fulfilment in a "civilization of love".

Hope

I wish to say to all, and especially to the young: never lose hope, the hope that comes from the Risen Christ, from God's victory over sin, hatred and death.

Today's Second Reading shows us precisely the final outcome of Jesus' Resurrection: it is the new Jerusalem, the Holy City that comes down from Heaven, from God, adorned as a bride for her husband (cf. *Rv* 21:2). The One who was crucified, who shared our suffering as the sacred Shroud also eloquently reminds us is the One who is Risen and who wants to reunite us all in his love. It is a marvellous, "strong" and solid hope, because, as Revelation says: "[God] will wipe away every tear from their eyes, and death shall be no more, neither shall there be mourning nor crying nor pain any more, for the former things have passed away" (21:4). Does not the Holy Shroud communicate the same message? In it we see, as in a mirror, our suffering in the suffering of Christ: *Passio Christi. Passio hominis.* For this very reason the Shroud is a sign of hope: Christ faced the Cross to stem evil; to make us see, in his Pasch, the anticipation of that moment when, even for us, every tear will be wiped away, when there will no longer be death, mourning or lamentation.

New things

The passage from Revelation ends with this assertion: "And he who sat upon the throne said: "Behold, I make all things new'" (21:5). The first absolutely new thing made by God was Jesus' Resurrection, his heavenly glorification. This is the beginning of a whole series of "new things" in which we also have a share. "New things" are a world full of joy, in which there is no more suffering and oppression, there is no more rancour or hate, but only the love that comes from God and transforms all things.

Dear Church in Turin, I have come to you to strengthen you in the faith. I would like to urge you, forcefully and with affection, to remain steadfast in that faith which you have received, that gives meaning to life and that gives the strength to love; never to lose the light of hope in the Risen Christ, who can transform reality and make all things new; to live out God's love in a simple, practical way in the City, in its districts, in communities, in families: "As I have loved you, that you also love one another". Amen.

Spiritual renewal

As we are about to conclude this solemn celebration, let us turn in prayer to Mary Most Holy, who is venerated in Turin as the principal Patron Saint, with the title of Our Lady Consolata. To her I entrust this city and all who live in it. O Mary, watch over the families and over the world of work. Watch over those who have lost their faith and hope. Comfort the sick, the prisoners and all the suffering. O Help of Christians, sustain the young, the elderly and people in difficulty. O Mother of the Church, watch over the Pastors and over the entire community of believers so that they may be "salt and light" in society.

The Virgin Mary is the one who, more than any other, contemplated God in the human face of Jesus. She saw him newborn, when she wrapped him in swaddling clothes and laid him in a manger; she saw him just after he died, when, having been taken down from the Cross, he was wrapped in a shroud and carried to the tomb. Impressed within her was the image of her tortured Son, but this image was subsequently transfigured by the light of the Resurrection. Thus, in Mary's heart the mystery of the Face of Christ was preserved a mystery of death and of glory. From her, we can always learn to look at Jesus with love and faith, and to see in that human face the Face of God.

With gratitude I entrust to the Most Holy Mother all who worked to prepare my Visit and for the Exposition of the Shroud. I pray for them and I pray that these events may promote a profound spiritual renewal.

True freedom: a view to the "forever"

I am truly glad to be with you on this Visit to Turin to Venerate the Holy Shroud. I greet all of you with great affection and I thank you for your welcome and the enthusiasm of your faith. Through you, I greet all the young people of Turin and of the Dioceses of Piedmont, with a special prayer for those who are in situations of suffering, difficulty or confusion. I address a special thought and strong encouragement to those of you who are following the path to the priesthood, to the consecrated life or to generous decisions in the service of the lowliest. I thank your Pastor, Cardinal Severino Poletto, for the cordial words he has addressed to me, and I thank your representatives who have presented to me the proposals, problems and expectations of the young people of this City and this region.

The rich young man

Twenty-five years ago, on the occasion of the World Youth Day, Venerable and Beloved John Paul II wrote an Apostolic Letter to the young people of the world, focused on Jesus' encounter with the rich young man in the Gospel (*Apostolic Letter to the Youth of the World*, 31 March 1985).

Precisely on the basis of this Gospel passage (cf. *Mk* 10:17-22; *Mt* 19:16-22) which was also the subject of my Reflection for this year's Message for the World Youth Day, I wish to offer some thoughts that I hope may help you in your spiritual growth and in your mission within the Church and in the world.

A special gift of yourselves

The young man in the Gospel as we know asks Jesus: "What must I do to inherit eternal life?". Today it is not easy to speak about eternal life and eternal realities, because the mentality of our time tells us that nothing is definitive that everything changes, and changes very rapidly. "Change", in many cases, has become the password, the most exalting exercise of freedom, and that is why even you, young people, have often come to think that it is impossible to make definitive choices that would tie you down for the rest of your life. But is this the right way to use your freedom? Is it really true that in order to be happy we should content ourselves with small, transient joys that once they are over leave bitterness in the heart? Dear young people, this is not true freedom nor can true happiness be reached in this way. Not one of us is created to make provisional and revocable choices but rather definitive and irrevocable decisions that give full meaning to our existence. We see it in our lives: we should like every beautiful experience that fills us with happiness never to end. God created us with a view to the "forever", he has placed in the heart of each one of us the seed of a life that can achieve something beautiful and great. Have the courage to make definitive decisions and to live them faithfully! The Lord may call you to marriage, to the priesthood, to the consecrated life, to a special gift of yourselves: answer him generously!

The greatest treasure in life

In the dialogue with the young man who possessed many riches Jesus pointed out what was the most important, the greatest treasure in life: love. To love God and to love others with one's whole self. The word love we know it lends itself to many interpretations and has different meanings. We need a Teacher, Christ, to teach us its most authentic and profound meaning, to guide us to the source of love and life. Love is the name of God himself. The Apostle John reminds us: "God is love", and adds, "not that we loved God but that he loved us and sent his Son", and "if God so loved us, we also ought to love one another" (1 *Jn* 4: 8,10-11) In the encounter with Christ and in reciprocal love we experience in ourselves the life of God, who abides in us with his perfect, total and eternal love (cf. 1 *Jn* 4:12). Therefore there is nothing greater for man a mortal and limited being than to participate in the life of God's love. Today, we live in a cultural context that does not encourage profound and disinterested human relationships; on the contrary, it often induces us to withdraw into ourselves, into individualism, to let selfishness, that exists in people, prevail. But a young person's heart is by nature sensitive to true love. That is why I address each one of you with great confidence in order to say: it is not easy to make something beautiful and great of your life it is demanding, but with Christ, everything is possible!

The gaze of Jesus

In the gaze of Jesus, who, as the Gospel tells us, looked lovingly at the young man, we perceive God's desire to be with us, to be near us. God desires our "yes", our love. Yes, dear young people, Jesus wants to be your friend, your brother in life, the teacher who shows you the way to follow to attain happiness. He loves you for what you are, in your frailty and your weakness, so that, touched by his love, you may be transformed. Live this encounter with Christ's love in a strong personal relationship with him. Live it in the Church, first and foremost in the Sacraments. Live it in the Eucharist, in which his Sacrifice is made present: he truly gives his Body and Blood for us, to redeem humanity's sins so that we may become one with him, so that we too may learn the logic of giving ourselves. Live it in Confession where, in offering us his forgiveness, Jesus accepts us with all our limitations in order to give us a new heart that can love as he does. Learn and become familiar with the word of God and meditate upon it, especially in *Lectio Divina*, the spiritual reading of the Bible. Lastly, learn to find Christ's love in the Church's testimony of charity. Turin's history offers you splendid examples: follow them, making a practical experience of service freely given. Everything in the ecclesial community should be aimed at making people feel tangibly the infinite charity of God.

Leaving behind the individualistic

Dear friends, Christ's love for the young man of the Gospel is the same love that he has for each one of you. It is not a love confined to the past, it is not an illusion, it is not reserved for a few. You will encounter this love and will experience all its fruitfulness if you seek the Lord sincerely and live with commitment your participation in the life of the Christian community. May each one of you feel "a living part" of the Church, engaging without fear in her work of evangelization, in a spirit of sincere harmony with your brothers and sisters in the faith and in communion with your Pastors, leaving behind every individualistic tendency, also in living out faith, in order to breathe deeply the beauty of being part of the great mosaic of Christ's Church.

Living, not just getting by

This evening I cannot fail to point out to you as a model a young man of your City Blessed Pier Giorgio Frassati, the 20th anniversary of whose Beatification falls this year. His life was completely enveloped by God's grace and love and was spent with serenity and joy in the enthusiastic service of Christ and of his brothers and sisters. Young like you, he experienced his Christian formation with deep commitment and gave his testimony of faith, simply and effectively. A young man who was drawn by the beauty of the Gospel of the Beatitudes, who experienced to the full the joy of being a friend of Christ, of following him, of feeling that he himself was a living part of the Church.

Dear young people, have the courage to choose what is essential in life! "Living, and not just managing to get by!", Blessed Pier Giorgio Frassati often used to say. Like him, you will discover that it is worth committing yourself to God and with God, to answer his call in your fundamental and your daily decisions, even at a cost!

The spiritual journey of Bl. Pier Giorgio Frassati reminds us that the journey of Christ's disciples demands the courage to come out of oneself, to follow the path of the Gospel.

The path of the spirit

You live this demanding path of the spirit in your parishes and in other ecclesial realities. You also live it during the pilgrimage of the World Youth Days, an event that is always eagerly awaited. I know that you are preparing for the next great meeting, scheduled to take place in Madrid in August 2011. I hope with all my heart that this extraordinary event, in which I hope that large numbers of you will participate, will help to increase in each one of you enthusiasm and faithfulness in following Christ and accepting his message with joy as the source of new life.

Witness

Young people of Turin and Piedmont, be witnesses of Christ in our time! May the Holy Shroud be an invitation, especially for you, to impress in your minds God's Face of love, so that you yourselves, in your own circles and among your contemporaries, may be a credible expression of the Face of Christ. May Mary, whom you venerate in your Marian shrines, and St John Bosco, Patron of young people, help you to follow Christ without ever tiring. May you always be accompanied by my prayers and my Blessing, which I impart to you with deep affection. Thank you for your attention!

An Icon written in blood

This is a moment to which I have been looking forward. I have stood before the Holy Shroud on various occasions but this time I am experiencing this Pilgrimage and this moment with special intensity: perhaps this is because the passing years make me even more sensitive to the message of this extraordinary Icon; perhaps and I would say above all this is because I am here now as the Successor of Peter, and I carry in my heart the whole Church, indeed, the whole of humanity. I thank God for the gift of this Pilgrimage and also for the opportunity to share with you a brief meditation inspired by the subtitle of this solemn Exposition: "The Mystery of Holy Saturday".

Mystery of Holy Saturday

One could say that the Shroud is the Icon of this mystery, the Icon of Holy Saturday. Indeed it is a winding-sheet that was wrapped round the body of a man who was crucified, corresponding in every way to what the Gospels tell us of Jesus who, crucified at about noon, died at about three o'clock in the afternoon. At nightfall, since it was *Parasceve*, that is, the eve of Holy Saturday, Joseph of Arimathea, a rich and authoritative member of the Sanhedrin, courageously asked Pontius Pilate for permission to bury Jesus in his new tomb which he had had hewn out in the rock not far from Golgotha. Having obtained permission, he bought a linen cloth, and after Jesus was taken down from the Cross, wrapped him in that shroud and buried him in that tomb (cf. *Mk* 15:42-46). This is what the Gospel of St Mark says and the other Evangelists are in agreement with him. From that moment, Jesus remained in the tomb until dawn of the day after the Sabbath and the Turin Shroud presents to us an image of how his body lay in the tomb during that period which was chronologically brief (about a day and a half), but immense, infinite in its value and in its significance.

Holy Saturday is the day when God remains hidden, we read in an ancient Homily: "What has happened? Today the earth is shrouded in deep silence, deep silence and stillness, profound silence because the King sleeps.... God has died in the flesh, and has gone down to rouse the realm of the dead" (*Homily on Holy Saturday*, PG 43, 439). In the *Creed*, we profess that Jesus Christ was "crucified under Pontius Pilate, died and was buried. He descended to the dead. On the third day, he rose again".

A void in the heart

Dear brothers and sisters, in our time, especially after having lived through the past century, humanity has become particularly sensitive to the mystery of Holy Saturday. The concealment of God is part of contemporary man's spirituality, in an existential almost subconscious manner, like a void in the heart that has continued to grow larger and larger. Towards the end of the 19th century, Nietzsche wrote: "God is dead! And we killed him!". This famous saying is clearly taken almost literally from the Christian tradition. We often repeat it in the Way of the Cross, perhaps without being fully aware of what we are saying. After the two World Wars, the lagers and the gulags, Hiroshima and Nagasaki, our epoch has become increasingly a Holy Saturday: this day's darkness challenges all who are wondering about life and it challenges us believers in particular. We too have something to do with this darkness.

Radical solidarity

Yet the death of the Son of God, Jesus of Nazareth, has an opposite aspect, totally positive, a source of comfort and hope. And this reminds me of the fact that the Holy Shroud acts as a "photographic' document, with both a "positive" and a "negative". And, in fact, this is really how it is: the darkest mystery of faith is at the same time the most luminous sign of a never-ending hope. Holy Saturday is a "no man's land" between the death and the Resurrection, but this "no man's land" was entered by One, the Only One, who passed through it with the signs of his Passion for man's sake: *Passio Christi. Passio hominis.* And the Shroud speaks to us precisely about this moment testifying exactly to that unique and unrepeatable interval in the history of humanity and the universe in which God, in Jesus Christ, not only shared our dying but also our remaining in death the most radical solidarity.

Love penetrated hell

In this "time-beyond-time", Jesus Christ "descended to the dead". What do these words mean? They mean that God, having made himself man, reached the point of entering man's most extreme and absolute solitude, where not a ray of love enters, where total abandonment reigns without any word of comfort: "hell". Jesus Christ, by remaining in death, passed beyond the door of this ultimate solitude to lead us too to cross it with him. We have all, at some point, felt the frightening sensation of abandonment, and that is what we fear most about death, just as when we were children we were afraid to be alone in the dark and could only be reassured by the presence of a person who loved us. Well, this is exactly what happened on Holy Saturday: the voice of God resounded in the realm of death. The unimaginable occurred: namely, Love penetrated "hell". Even in the extreme darkness of the most absolute human loneliness we may hear a voice that calls us and find a hand that takes ours and leads us out. Human beings live because they are loved and can love; and if love even penetrated the realm of death, then life also even reached there. In the hour of supreme solitude we shall never be alone: *Passio Christi. Passio hominis.*

Light of the Resurrection

This is the mystery of Holy Saturday! Truly from there, from the darkness of the death of the Son of God, the light of a new hope gleamed: the light of the Resurrection. And it seems to me that, looking at this sacred Cloth through the eyes of faith, one may perceive something of this light. Effectively, the Shroud was immersed in that profound darkness that was at the same time luminous; and I think that if thousands and thousands of people come to venerate it without counting those who contemplate it through images it is because they see in it not only darkness but also the light; not so much the defeat of life and of love, but rather victory, the victory of life over death, of love over hatred. They indeed see the death of Jesus, but they also see his Resurrection; in the bosom of death, life is now vibrant, since love dwells within it.

The passion of mankind

This is the power of the Shroud: from the face of this "Man of sorrows", who carries with him the passion of man of every time and every place, our passions too, our sufferings, our difficulties and our sins *Passio Christi. Passio hominis* from this face a solemn majesty shines, a paradoxical lordship. This face, these hands and these feet, this side, this whole body speaks. It is itself a word we can hear in the silence. How does the Shroud speak? It speaks with blood, and blood is life! The Shroud is an Icon written in blood; the blood of a man who was scourged, crowned with thorns, crucified and whose right side was pierced. The Image impressed upon the Shroud is that of a dead man, but the blood speaks of his life. Every trace of blood speaks of love and of life. Especially that huge stain near his rib, made by the blood and water that flowed copiously from a great wound inflicted by the tip of a Roman spear. That blood and that water speak of life. It is like a spring that murmurs in the silence, and we can hear it, we can listen to it in the silence of Holy Saturday.

Faith, hope and charity

Dear friends, let us always praise the Lord for his faithful and merciful love. When we leave this holy place, may we carry in our eyes the image of the Shroud, may we carry in our hearts this word of love and praise God with a life full of faith, hope and charity. Thank you.

Suffering and redemption

I would like to express to all of you my joy and gratitude to the Lord who has brought me here to you, to this place where the love and Providence of the heavenly Father are expressed in so many ways and in accordance with a special charism. Our meeting is one which is in harmony with my Pilgrimage to the Holy Shroud, in it not only can we interpret the whole drama of suffering but also, in the light of Christ's Resurrection, its full meaning for the world's redemption.

St Joseph Benedict Cottolengo

I thank Fr Aldo Sarotto for his meaningful words to me: through him I extend my thanks to all who work in this place, the Little House of Divine Providence, as St Joseph Benedict Cottolengo chose to call it. I greet with gratitude the three religious families born from Cottolengo's heart and from the "imagination" of the Holy Spirit. Thanks to all of you, dear sick people, who are the precious treasure of this house and of this Institution.

As you may know, at the General Audience last Wednesday, together with the figure of St Leonard Murialdo, I also presented your Founder's charism and work. Yes, he was a true and proper champion of charity whose initiatives, like flourishing trees, stand before our eyes and before the gaze of the world.

Scourge of poverty

In re-reading the testimonies of that time, we note that it was far from easy for Cottolengo to begin his undertaking. The many activities of social assistence that existed for the neediest in the area did not suffice to heal the scourge of poverty that afflicted the city of Turin. St Cottolengo sought to respond to this situation by taking in people in difficulty and giving priority to those who were not accepted and cared for by others. The first nucleus of the House of Divine Providence experienced hardship and did not last long. In 1832, a new structure in the Valdocco district to which several religious families also gave a helping hand came into being.

The poor are Jesus

In spite of going through dramatic moments in his life, St Cottolengo always kept his serene trust in the face of events; attentive to perceiving the signs of God's fatherhood, he recognized his presence and his mercy in every situation and, in the poor, the most lovable image of his greatness. He was guided by a deep conviction: "The poor are Jesus" he used to say, "they are not just an image of him. They are Jesus in person and must be served as such. All the poor are our masters, but these who look so repulsive to the physical eye are even more particularly our masters, they are our true jewels. If we do not treat them well, let them chase us out of the Little House. They are Jesus".

Motivated in the depths of his heart by the Apostle Paul's words: *the love of Christ impels us* (cf. 2 *Co* 5:14), St Joseph Benedict Cottolengo felt he should work both for God and for man. He wanted to express this in unreserved dedication to the service of the smallest and the most forsaken. From the outset, a fundamental principle of his work was the exercise of Christian charity for all. This permitted him to recognize great dignity in every person, even those on the fringes of society.

Family style

Cottolengo had understood that those hit by suffering and rejection tend to withdraw and isolate themselves and to express distrust of life itself. Thus, for our Saint, taking on the burden of so much human suffering meant creating relations of affective, family and spontaneous closeness by opening establishments that would favour this closeness in that family style which still endures today.

Personal dignity

For St Joseph Benedict Cottolengo, the recovery of personal dignity meant re-establishing and appreciating the whole human being: from his fundamental psychological, social needs to his moral and spiritual needs, from the rehabilitation of his physical functions to the search for a meaning to life, bringing the person to feel that he/she was still a living part of the ecclesial community and of the ecclesial fabric. We are grateful to this great apostle of charity because in visiting these places, in encountering the daily suffering in the faces and limbs of so many of our brothers and sisters, accepted here as in their own homes, we may experience the deepest value and meaning of suffering and pain.

Mystery of suffering

Dear sick people, you are carrying out an important activity: by living your suffering in union with the Crucified and Risen Christ, you share in the mystery of his suffering for the world's salvation. By offering our pain to God through Christ, we can collaborate in the victory of good over evil, because God makes our offering, our act of love fruitful. Dear brothers and sisters, all of you who are here, may each one for his own part: do not feel irrelevant to the world's future but rather feel that you are precious pieces of a most beautiful mosaic that God, like a great artist, continues to create day by day, also with your contribution. Christ, who died on the Cross to save us, let himself be nailed to it so that life in its full splendour might blossom from that wood, from that sign of death. This house is one of the ripe fruits that the Cross and Resurrection of Christ have produced and shows that suffering, evil and death do not have the last word, for life can be reborn from death and suffering. One of you, whom I wish to remember witnessed to this in an exemplary way: Venerable Bro. Luigi Bordino, a marvellous religious who was also a nurse.

Nothing lost in the light of his Face

In this place, then, we understand better that since the human passion was taken on by Christ in his Passion, nothing will be lost. The message of this solemn Exposition of the Holy Shroud: *Passio Christi - Passio hominis*, may be understood here in a special way. Let us pray the Crucified and Risen Lord that he may illumine our daily pilgrimage with the light of his Face: may he illumine our lives, the present and the future, the anguish and the joy and the struggles and the hopes of all of humanity. I cordially impart my Blessing to you all, dear brothers and sisters, as I invoke the intercession of the Virgin Mary and St Joseph Benedict Cottolengo: may it comfort and console you in trials and obtain for you every grace that comes from God, the author and giver of every perfect gift. Thank you!

Sources

This booklet draws together homilies and addresses of Pope Benedict XVI, made during his Pastoral Visit to Turin, 2 May 2010:

A civilization of love: Eucharistic celebration - homily of his Holiness Benedict XVI, St Charles Square, Fifth Sunday of Easter, 2 May 2010.

Spiritual renewal: Benedict XVI - Regina Caeli, St Charles Square, Fifth Sunday of Easter, 2 May 2010.

True freedom: a view to the "forever": Meeting with the young people - address of his Holiness Benedict XVI, St Charles Square, Fifth Sunday of Easter, 2 May 2010.

An Icon written in blood: Veneration of the holy shroud - meditation of his Holiness Benedict XVI, St Charles Square, Fifth Sunday of Easter, 2 May 2010.

Suffering and redemption: Meeting with the sick – address of his Holiness Benedict XVI, Church of the Little House of Divine Providence – Cottolengo, Fifth Sunday of Easter, 2 May 2010.